ACTION GUIDE
FOR
Effective Fathers

TYNDALE HOUSE
PUBLISHERS, INC.
WHEATON, ILLINOIS

Acknowledgments
Grateful acknowledgment is given to Campus Crusade for Christ, International
(The Four Spiritual Laws), *and Inter Varsity Press (Paul Little,* How to Give
Away Your Faith) *for the basic principles of the gospel presentation.*

Bible quotations in this book are taken from *The Living Bible* or the *Revised
Standard Version.*

Library of Congress Catalog Card Number 79-89069
ISBN 0-8423-0688-9, paper
Second printing, January 1980.
Printed in the United States of America.

CONTENTS

FOREWORD 5
PREFACE 7
NOTE TO THE DISCUSSION LEADER 9
INTRODUCTION 11
    1   "One Very Human Shortcoming" 11

FIRST PRINCIPLE 17
    2   "It's Not a Phony War" 19
    3   I Accept the Mandate 23
    4   Is There a Price to Pay? 27

SECOND PRINCIPLE 35
    5   Setting the Pace; Beating the Tempo 37
    6   A Fountain of Life 39
    7   No Day Is Ever Wasted 45
    8   Fragile: Handle with Care 53
    9   Wear Shoes You Want Filled 57
    10   No Busy Signals Here 63

THIRD PRINCIPLE 73
    11   Life in White Water 75

FOURTH PRINCIPLE 85
    12   To Raise a Great Cathedral 87

FIFTH PRINCIPLE 101
    13   Please Show Me That You Care 103

SIXTH PRINCIPLE 111
    14   The Sour Hour—The Ineffective Father 113

FOREWORD

Being an effective father or mother depends upon spiritual commitment, hard work, and lots of wisdom. Those who depend upon brilliance, material acquisition and accumulation, or brute force need not apply. That's what I've reaffirmed after having read scores of letters written by men and women from all over the world who have read the book *The Effective Father*.

And that's why I am overjoyed by the publication of the companion action guide which can now be used by TEF readers. It has been designed by Christian men who believe in the priority of effective fathers and who have devised ways in which each of us can creatively think through the most basic issues of raising children in this age.

One discovery they've made that excites me is that both TEF and the action guide are helpful to women who want to think through their effectiveness as mothers. Used by men and women as a personal resource or by groups as a discussion agenda, the companion action guide to TEF has already caused many to rethink the ways in which their families are living and growing.

I suspect that the action guide could be a bit dangerous for those who try not to face the facts of parenting squarely. It has a way of causing one to turn up patterns and convictions of living that are painful to deal with. But for those with a bit of courage and desire to grow as a parent, it becomes just the right tool to give appropriate assistance and encouragement.

I'm delighted with and thankful for the work that Pat McMillan, Jim Webb, and Bob Buechner have done in this action book. I see God speaking through them, and I believe that their work will lead many of us toward a higher effectiveness in this great business of being a parent.

Gordon MacDonald

PREFACE

For eight weeks, twelve men met for an hour and a half every Saturday morning to discuss the issues confronting us as fathers and the principles identified by Gordon MacDonald in his book, *The Effective Father*.

We found that meeting over this eight-week period of time not only disciplined our reading but that the discussion, prayer, and encouragement of the other men greatly increased the degree of application of these principles to our personal lives. The book is uniquely written in that it is a sharing experience rather than another "manual" for lost parents. MacDonald himself notes that the focus is "identification rather than instruction, challenge rather than correction." Its informal, warm, and flowing style is very conducive to discussion. It was almost as though the author was part of our Saturday morning group. As these men shared their own experiences, the result was an even greater degree of richness to the material—a greater dimension of understanding and application.

The word spread. Others asked to join the group and to be a part of new ones. It was obvious that this book—its content and style—was addressing a very critical and unmet need with the fathers in our area. As the groups expanded, it became necessary to write down the study questions that were found to be the most relevant in order to allow expansion of these groups. These notes utimately led to the development of this action guide.

The purpose of this discussion manual is to facilitate application of the material and principles shared by Gordon MacDonald in *The Effective Father*. This is done by highlighting key points found in each of the chapters and presenting questions designed to help us evaluate our personal situation as it relates to a specific principle. The questions are designed to stimulate group discussion of the material and help us tie down specific actions we will incorporate into our task of fatherhood to allow us to become more effective fathers.

This book can be used in several ways, either as a workbook for individual study, or as a discussion guide to facilitate group interaction and discussion.

We want to encourage you to consider starting or being part of a discussion group. When several men get together to study and discuss the material, understanding increases significantly. Not only does the group dynamic enhance the learning experience, but the group provides a base of support and encouragement as the men begin to apply these key concepts and principles to their families.

If a discussion group approach is used, the following section will provide some direction as to format, schedule, and procedures.

The focus must be on application. Only as we turn principle into practice will we become effective fathers. This effectiveness will be demonstrated by the lives of our children, not just by the knowledge in our head. We pray that you find this material helpful and that these discussion sessions are as meaningful to you as they have been to us.

For further information
on the use of this study, write:
Effective Father Ministries
Post Office Box 98311
Atlanta, Georgia 30359

NOTE TO THE DISCUSSION LEADER

The objective of these notes is to explain the purpose of the group and your role as discussion leader; and to share a few points that will make your task easier and more successful.

Your position as discussion leader does not cast you in the role of "having arrived" as an effective father, with principles in hand. Instead, it identifies you as someone committed to the concept of *becoming* an effective father.

The purpose of the discussion group is to create an atmosphere for learning. The interaction in this group provides an additional dimension to the learning process, with the result of increased application.

This is a book of principles—intangible tools we can use to build our children. But as with any tool, our skill in using it plays a major role in the ultimate outcome. Skill is a function of both knowledge and experience or practice. Gordon MacDonald's book, in sharing the principles, provides the knowledge. The discussion group provides a creative way for us to quickly broaden our base of experience. The group can provide through its interaction insights to creative application, ways that work and don't work, confirmation of direction and the need for change.

As group leader, you are not a lecturer or teacher, but a discussion leader. Your role is to be a facilitator, a helper —to keep the discussion flowing, redirect it if it gets off course, sum up group conclusions, and focus on an application.

The discussion questions for each session have been designed to highlight the key points, identify individual needs, and help us work through specific application of that particular principle or concept. It's important that you do your "homework" before each session, reading the assigned materials and answering the discussion questions pertinent to that section. These are not the "right answers" or even all-inclusive, but merely some possibilities for you to use *if* discussion lags or gets off course.

The format is very simple. We found that the optimum length for a session was approximately one and a half to two hours. This allowed time for some coffee and fellowship, discussion of the questions, sharing of discoveries as we applied these principles to our day-to-day family activities, and closing prayer. Prior to the session, each man was responsible to read the week's assignment and work through his individual response to the discussion questions. You may want to break down your session as follows:

15–20 minutes	Coffee and fellowship ★ Open in prayer.
45–60 minutes	Discussion ★ Share application from previous sessions. ★ Discussion questions.
10–15 minutes	Action point ★ Five minutes to think through personal application. ★ Ten minutes to share point with others.
10–15 minutes	Prayer

Group size varies, but should range from six to twelve people. If a group gets much larger, intimacy is lost; if it is too small, the group's dynamic lessens.

Prior to starting a discussion series, it would be good to send a note to each individual in the group. The purpose is to welcome each person to the group, remind him of time and location, tell him where he can obtain the book and discussion guide, and assign him the initial reading. This way, most men will attend the first session "ready to go."

INTRODUCTION

1 *"One Very Human Shortcoming"*

Reading Assignment:

Introduction	"I Had Always Taught Our Children"
Chapter 1	"One Very Human Shortcoming"

Session Objectives:

To Get to Know One Another

To Establish the Need to Develop Effective Leadership in Your Home

To Preview the Course; Its Purpose, Scope, and Method

NOTES AND COMMENTS

♦ "Perhaps the place to begin a definition of effective leadership is with the recognition that there is need for order in family relationships before God and the surrounding community. People living in proximity to one another have to be placed in some design or there will be conflict and chaos. Disordered families create disordered communities" (p. 23).

_____

_____

_____

_____

_____

_____

_____

♦ "In its positive sense, effective leadership is designed to bring people to maturity, to the ultimate reaches of their human potential" (p. 23).

_____

_____

_____

_____

_____

♦ "In the negative perspective, effective leadership is the enforcement of order when there is unwillingness to fit into the process of relationships, an attitude that makes life miserable for everyone" (p. 23).

_____

_____

_____

_____

1. In the Introduction Gordon MacDonald notes that "it is the father who is required to create delicate conditions in which a child grows to be a man or woman, to attain the fullness of all that human potential that God has designed" (p. 15).

   Briefly list some of the conditions you feel are needed in order that your children can maximize their potential.

   _____

   _____

   _____

   _____

2. Take a few moments and list some of the attributes and character traits you desire your children to have spiritually, socially, mentally, physically when they are eighteen years old.

   _____

   _____

   _____

   _____

   _____

3. Briefly list the characteristics you feel an effective father must have. Circle the one you feel is the most important.

   _____   _____

   _____   _____

   _____   _____

NOTES AND COMMENTS

◆ "If the family is a group of human beings so tied together, it is the father who is the knot where the ends of the laces meet" (p. 25).

_____

_____

_____

_____

_____

_____

_____

_____

_____

_____

_____

_____

_____

_____

_____

_____

_____

_____

_____

_____

_____

4. Can you identify your three greatest strengths as a father?

_____

_____

_____

5. What are your three major weaknesses as a father?

_____

_____

_____

6. What three objectives do you hope to accomplish from these sessions over the next eight weeks?

_____

_____

_____

_____

_____

_____

_____

_____

_____

FIRST PRINCIPLE

If I am an effective father . . . it is because I have deliberately set as one of my life's highest priorities the creation of conditions in my home that will stimulate my children to grow to their full human potential.

Reading Assignment:

Chapter 2   "It's Not a Phony War"
Chapter 3   I Accept the Mandate
Chapter 4   Is There a Price to Pay?

Session Objectives:

To Identify the Secular and Spiritual Elements in the War for the Spirits of My Children.
To Understand God's Mandate to Us As Fathers.
To Determine the Price of Being an Effective Father.

NOTES AND COMMENTS

_____

_____

_____

_____

♦ "Naturally, civilization isn't all evil, and the amount of reality in the world to discover and enjoy is mind-expanding. But the father who hasn't perceived that life in this age is much like crossing a mine field during a war, had better prepare himself for some heavy casualties" (p. 32).

_____

_____

_____

_____

_____

_____

_____

_____

_____

_____

_____

_____

_____

_____

_____

_____

_____

2 *"It's Not a Phony War"*

This chapter talks about a war—a real war raging around our families. Do you believe this? Yes □ No □ I'm not sure □ Convince me! □

1. Who are the contestants of this war? _____

_____

_____

2. What is the prize, the objective of the war? _____

_____

_____

3. What is my responsibility, as the father, in this war? __

_____

_____

_____

4. Take a few moments and look up the following Scripture verses.
   Ephesians 6:12. Our struggle is against _____

_____

_____

2 Corinthians 2:11b; Ephesians 6:11. We are:
1. _____
2. _____

_____

1 Peter 5:8, 9a. What actions does Peter admonish us to take?
1. _____
2. _____
3. _____

_____

NOTES AND COMMENTS

_____

_____

_____

_____

_____

_____

_____

_____

_____

_____

_____

_____

_____

_____

_____

◗ In 2 Corinthians 11:14, Paul notes that Satan disguises himself as an angel of light. This possibility makes the situation even more dangerous—light not only provides direction but attracts. Could it be that some of the mines or explosive devices of this war are disguised as something else? Something which looks harmless or even good and desirable . . . on the surface?

_____

_____

_____

_____

_____

_____

_____

5. MacDonald applies his spiritual mine detector and identifies a number of things capable of exploding in a family's face. Take a few moments and apply this detector to your own family situation.

	Not applicable. Check back in a few years.	I've heard it's in the area but hasn't made its appearance.	Periodic sightings but no contact yet.	I can smell smoke but there's no fire.	I smell something burning . . .	HELP!
Newspapers, periodicals, etc.						
Television, radio, movies, music, etc.						
My personal schedule—"absent too much"; "quantity but not quality."						
School activities, extra curricular activities, etc.						
The effect of affluence						
Peer group influence						
Other: _____						

Which is the most potentially dangerous item in the above list at the present time? _____

How is it making its influence known? _____

_____

NOTES AND COMMENTS

_____

_____

_____

_____

_____

_____

_____

_____

_____

_____

_____

_____

_____

_____

_____

_____

_____

_____

◗ "Effective fatherhood has something to do with a way of life. Call it—according to Moses' approach—saturation leadership" (p. 45).

_____

_____

_____

_____

_____

_____

_____

6. How will you diffuse this threat? _____

_____

7. MacDonald also mentioned a number of ways fathers use to cope with this war—building protective walls, establishing rigid rules, the laissez-faire attitude. What are some less extreme, more creative ideas as to how to defuse these mines?

_____

_____

_____

8. How do you think Romans 12:2 applies to this war and mine field?

_____

_____

3 I Accept the Mandate

The first principle concerns creating conditions that will stimulate our children to grow to their full human potential. Maintaining these conditions (climate of environment) requires *constant monitoring* of temperature, humidity, pressure, etc., with *quick adjustments* to maintain maximum standards—the best environment.

Thus MacDonald concludes that "effective fatherhood is a preoccupying way of life."

He points out that God has given us both a mandate and a set of directions for maintaining this environment—these conditions.

Hear O Israel: The Lord our God is one Lord; and you shall love the Lord your God with all your heart, and with all your soul, and with all your might. And

NOTES AND COMMENTS

_____

_____

_____

_____

_____

_____

_____

_____

_____

_____

_____

_____

◆ "The challenge is in saturating the routine of normal living with the plan and the presence of God. In short, insure that life within your home is so positive, so appealing, so fulfilling that all else in the outside world pales in contrast to what a child receives when he is with the family" (pp. 45, 46).

_____

_____

_____

_____

_____

_____

_____

_____

_____

_____

these words which I command you this day shall be upon your heart; and you shall *teach* them diligently to your children, and shall *talk* of them when you *sit* in your house, and when you *walk* by the way, and when you *lie down*, and when *you rise*. And you shall bind them as a sign upon your hand, and they shall be as frontlets between your eyes. And you shall *write them* on the doorposts of your house and on your gates (Deuteronomy 6:4-9).

The two active dimensions to Moses' charge to Israel's fathers are "teach" and "talk."

"In line with the first word, Moses apparently feels that there are times when a father deliberately sits down with his kids and imparts factual information that they need to have. The family altar kind of thing" (p. 46).

1. Do you have these times with your kids? _____

2. How often do you feel this type of interaction is needed? _____

3. What is the greatest obstacle confronting you, as a father, in having these times (quantitatively and qualitatively)? _____

"The second word is *talk*. And that takes place in the context of the ordinary routine. I think Moses is telling the effective father to carry on a running commentary with his children about the "whys" and "wherefores" of each event during the day. When a situation arises that might normally pave the way for a blowup of temper, that's a time to point out to a child why self-control is important and how it is achieved (provided, of course, *you* have achieved it)" (p. 46).

4. Do you have these "talks" with your kids? _____

NOTES AND COMMENTS

_____

_____

_____

_____

_____

_____

_____

_____

_____

_____

◗ "Big returns never happen in the future unless sizable investments are made in the present" (p. 50).

_____

_____

_____

_____

_____

_____

_____

_____

_____

_____

_____

_____

_____

_____

5. What is the major barrier to having these talks? _____

_____

6. What specifically is Moses telling us to teach our children and to talk to them about? _____

_____

7. Look up Joshua 1:8; Psalm 1:2, 3; 119:9, 11, 98, 105. What are some benefits to our children if they delight in God's Word?

_____

_____

_____

4 Is There a Price to Pay?

Yes!—with payment in advance.

MacDonald points out a few of the costs in his own life. Take a few moments and examine the price tag from your perspective.

ITEM 1 Personal discretionary freedoms	Leisure time, "your" TV programs, conversation and vocabulary, eating privileges, projects, reading, social activities, church and community activities, habits.

1. Reflect on these "discretionary freedoms," adding others that may not have been included. Any areas in which a price has to be paid to make you an effective father in your family? _____

_____

_____

NOTES AND COMMENTS

_____

_____

_____

_____

_____

◆ "Don't pick up that mandate unless you're willing to pay the price. It's a big one, and it is the reason why there are so few effective fathers" (p. 55).

_____

_____

_____

_____

_____

_____

_____

_____

_____

_____

_____

_____

_____

_____

_____

_____

_____

_____

ITEM 2
Concept of Success

There are as many definitions of success as people, and many different items are incorporated into these definitions. Some might include: God, personal development, spiritual growth, family, wealth, community position, social recognition, possessions, profession, creative achievements, etc.

2. Write out your present definition of success. _____
_____
_____

3. Do you see the need for any changes? _____

4. In what areas? _____
_____

ITEM 3
Letting God shape me
into the man he wants me
to be.

5. "Submitting to the hand of God upon my life" (p. 54).
   What does this mean to you? _____
   _____

6. Read Romans 12:1, 2. How do these verses apply to
   this area? _____
   _____
   _____

7. What are some other costs that might apply to this
   mandate? _____
   _____

NOTES AND COMMENTS

8. What are the returns on this investment? _____

_____

9. For me personally, the price of being an effective father
   is _____

_____

_____

_____

_____

I am willing to pay this price! To deliberately set
as one of my life's highest priorities the creation of
conditions in my home that will stimulate my children to grow to their full human potential.

_____   _____
         Signature   Date

To change priorities, direction, and approach in our family responsibilities is a major undertaking under the best of
circumstances. Regardless of our motivation and commitment to make these changes, many barriers will arise. A
few examples might include habit patterns, lack of time,
defensive attitudes, lack of knowledge, and our natural desire to serve our needs rather than the needs of others.

Also we must remember that many of the desired results
will occur not only because of our commitment to and application of these principles. Our success will be deter-
mined to some extent by the cooperation of our wives and
the response of our children, over which we have little
control.

Don't get discouraged—there's an answer. As Christians,
our limitation is our strength. See Luke 18:27. Christ said,
"The things impossible with men are possible with God."

NOTES AND COMMENTS

The apostle noted in his letter, 1 John 5:14, 15, "And this is the confidence which we have in him, that if we ask anything according to his will he hears us. And if we know that he hears us in whatever we ask, we know that we have obtained the requests made of him."

At the end of each session you will have a chance not only to clearly spell out the specific action you want to take in light of what you have learned, but you will have an opportunity to articulate in written form your desires to God—"What is your prayer concerning this issue?" This is a partnership: your willingness, plus God's power.

Dear Lord,

_____

_____

_____

_____

_____

_____

Signature

SECOND PRINCIPLE

If I am an effective father . . . it is because I have devoted myself to become an instrument and model of human experience to my children.

Reading Assignment:

Chapter 5   Setting the Pace; Beating the Tempo
Chapter 6   A Fountain of Life
Chapter 7   No Day Is Ever Wasted
Chapter 8   Fragile: Handle with Care
Chapter 9   Wear Shoes You Want Filled
Chapter 10   No Busy Signals Here

Session Objectives:

To identify the components of family leadership.

To understand some of the principles of effective communication.

To establish the importance of instruction and to identify creative methods of teaching our children.

To discover the key elements and principles of healthy verbal correction.

To establish the importance of modeling lifestyle and to identify some of the underlying principles of such modeling.

To learn the elements of being an "approachable" father.

NOTES AND COMMENTS

◆ "Without the conductor, the finest musicians and the most expensive instruments produce only inartistic chaos" (p. 60).

◆ "Jesus kept increasing in wisdom [mentally] and stature [physically] and in favor with God [spiritually] and men [socially]."

---

5 Setting the Pace; Beating the Tempo

This chapter establishes the need for effective leadership in the family. Gordon MacDonald explains that one reason good leadership is needed is "because individuals tend to be rebellious toward meaningful and costly relationships" (p. 60).

Do you agree with this? Yes ☐ No ☐ Don't get so personal. ☐

1. What can you do to consciously set the pace and tempo in your family?

   _____

   _____

2. We are introduced to two fathers in the Bible which provide us with a vivid example of the extremes of family leadership. Mordecai and Eli—both were aware of their children's situation. *Contrast the means by which they came to this awareness* (Esther 2:11; 1 Samuel 2:22).
   Mordecai: _____
   Eli: _____

3. "A pacesetter *knows* where the cars are, and the conductor *knows* the moment a musician is out of tempo or what instrument is not properly tuned" (p. 63).

   What application do you see in this analogy for your family?

   _____

   _____

   There is a popular public service television ad; "It's 10:00 P.M., do you know where your children are?" It refers to their physical location, but the same question can be applied to other dimensions of our children's lives—spiritual, social, moral, mental, etc.

NOTES AND COMMENTS

4. Are you able to *accurately* assess where your children are in these areas?

_____

5. Do you know where they *should be?* _____

_____

6. How could you make such an assessment? _____

_____

_____

Gordon MacDonald, in introducing the next four chapters, notes that this leadership may be exercised in a number of ways:

A. Through our words .... chapter 6
B. By precedents we set in daily
   instruction .... chapter 7
C. By the types of corrections we impose in
   ambiguous situations .... chapter 8

6 A Fountain of Life

"The mouth of the righteous is a
fountain of life . . ."
Proverbs 10:11.

In concluding the last chapter, MacDonald characterized the kind of pacesetting we're talking about with two words—initiate and motivate.

In introducing this chapter he notes, "A father *initiates action* in his family *through words*, and he *motivates* continuous action through words" (p. 69).

NOTES AND COMMENTS

1. "Words have an awesome impact. They can build, or they can destroy" (p. 67). What specific circumstances or situations in your home are conducive to the generation of *negative* words?

_____

_____

_____

_____

2. What action can you take to change or improve these situations? _____

_____

_____

_____

3. This chapter mentions three ground rules for effective verbal communication. Can you identify them?

   A. _____

   _____

   B. _____

   _____

   C. _____

   _____

   Basically, MacDonald is explaining that there are three elements in your communication process—a clear-cut signal, response time, and follow-through. In which of these areas would you rate yourself the strongest?

   _____

   The weakest? _____

   _____

4. Read 1 Corinthians 14:7-9. To which of our communication ground rules might it apply?

   _____

   _____

NOTES AND COMMENTS

5. Turn to page 73—carefully read and *underline* the second paragraph. Does this paragraph describe your communications with your children?

   Yes ☐ No ☐ I plan to start immediately. ☐

6. In discussing the need for follow-through, MacDonald identifies several types of fathers who "don't." Using only one sentence, describe these fathers.

   A. Dishonest father _____
   _____
   _____

   B. Threatening father _____
   _____
   _____

   C. Exploding father _____
   _____
   _____

   D. Silent father _____
   _____
   _____

7. Do you sometimes fall into any of these categories?
   Yes ☐ No ☐ I take the fifth amendment. ☐
   If yes, which one? _____
   If no, carefully reread chapter. ☐

8. What *specific action* will you take *this week* to become a more effective communicator to your family?

   _____
   _____
   _____
   _____
   _____
   _____
   _____

NOTES AND COMMENTS

7 *No Day Is Ever Wasted*

> "The teaching of the wise is a
> fountain of life"
>   Proverbs 13:14.

"Each day the effective father stamps into the lives of his children words, attitudes, habits, and responses which one day will become automatic . . . Ironically, teaching can be done either through design or neglect. Teaching, conscious or unconscious, will make an indelible impression upon a child's personality and become part of a composite of future character performance. The weaknesses and flaws of the father will be passed on to the children in either case" (p. 80).

Do you agree with this? Yes ☐ No ☐ Let's come back to this one later. ☐

1. Can you recall one specific example where you have *consciously taught* your children a certain attitude, habit, or response?

   _____

   _____

2. Can you recall an instance when they have learned or "picked up" a *negative* attitude, habit, or response in which your role was more passive or *unconscious?*

   _____

   _____

   _____

MacDonald distinguishes between *attitudes and values* and *abilities and performance*. This chapter focuses on the latter, which can be deliberately taught through positive planning of family experience.

NOTES AND COMMENTS

_____

_____

♦ "There aren't many fathers who can master all skills and arts. That's why a man deliberately exposes his children to as many other kinds of men as possible" (p. 82).

_____

_____

_____

_____

_____

_____

_____

_____

_____

_____

_____

♦ "Sharing with children _how_ things are done is not enough. Relationships in the context of work are important also" (p. 83).

_____

_____

_____

_____

_____

_____

_____

3. On the top of page 81 we are asked a provocative question: How does a child discover his or her abilities, gifts, and capacities and then put them to work?

   A. _____

   B. _____

   C. _____

   D. _____

4. One possible answer to the above question is to have them assist you with family responsibilities. In discussing an example (the repairing of a bicycle), MacDonald lists three possible reactions to such an opportunity—the lazy father, the busy father, or the wise father—which of these *most typically* characterizes your response?

   _____

5. Reflect for a moment on Boswell's reflections on his time with his father and the impact of this time on his life. Think through where your kids are getting their teaching (values, skills, and knowledge) and *contrast* this to where they are spending their time.

   By teaching, we mean both direct teaching and indirect modeling. As to the time, consider an average week, integrating the weekend and weekday time. This question takes time and thought but will provide valuable insight. Here again, answers will vary depending on each child and his age.

   Evaluate on a scale of 1-10 (1 is low, 10 is high). For example, if you feel that your children get approximately a third of their teaching from you, the father, but only spend a small part of their total time with you (e.g., 10 percent) then you might enter a 3 & 1 respectively on the first line. Remember this is only an approximation and a subjective one at that.

NOTES AND COMMENTS

_____

_____

_____

_____

_____

_____

_____

_____

_____

_____

_____

_____

_____

_____

_____

▶ "When the doors to a child's mind are open, he is probably ready for any kind of experience of learning his parents want him to have. When the doors are closed, teaching a child will be like trying to jam things through the crack at the bottom" (p. 84).

_____

_____

_____

_____

_____

_____

_____

_____

	TEACHING Where or from whom do your children learn? Approximate on a scale of 1-10.	*TIME* Where or with whom do your children spend their time? Again, express your estimate on a scale of 1-10.
Father		
Mother		
Father and mother as couple (team)		
School		
Peer group		
Other individuals		
Media (TV, magazines, etc.)		
Other		
TOTAL		

A. Does the above profile highlight the need for any changes in either the place where the learning is taking place or how the time is spent? If so, *specifically* what changes?

_____

B. Remember the old adage, "It's not the quantity of time that counts, but the quality of time."

Does this apply to the profile on the previous page? Yes ☐ No ☐

Don't rush me, I'm still trying to add up the columns. ☐

Are there limits to the application of this saying? ___

_____

Does the profile give us insight on this concept? ___

_____

NOTES AND COMMENTS

C. Which of the items on the above profile exercise a disproportionate amount of influence in relation to their time? _____

_____

Is this a positive or negative influence? _____

_____

Why do you think this is so? _____

_____

6. "There is a further capacity which must be mastered in the classroom of the family. Call it the teachable moment. We rarely *create* them; rather, we *sense* them" (p. 84.)

   Read this section carefully. What are the signals your children give that alert you to a *teachable moment?* Remember, the signals vary with each child.

   Child _____ _____

   _____

   _____

   _____ _____

   _____

   _____

   _____ _____

   _____

   _____

7. Want to gain an interesting insight? Turn back to question 5 and have your wife answer those questions.

8. Identify one *specific* item you've learned from this chapter and in no more than two sentences explain how you will apply this lesson with your family this coming week.

   _____

   _____

   _____

   _____

NOTES AND COMMENTS

8 *Fragile: Handle with Care*

> "Fathers, do not provoke your children to anger, but bring them up in the discipline and instruction of the Lord"
>
> Ephesians 6:4.

1. Above Paul admonishes us as fathers not to provoke our children to anger. In Colossians 3:21, he describes the consequence of doing so. What is this possible consequence?

   _____

2. The focus on this chapter deals with the "rebuke." How does MacDonald define a "rebuke"?

   _____
   _____

3. Using God's rebuke of Cain as an example (p. 89), MacDonald highlights the three elements of a healthy rebuke. Carefully read his explanation and list these three points below:

   A. _____
   B. _____
   C. _____

4. Does this describe the way you rebuke your children?

   Yes ☐ No ☐ The Spirit is willing, but the flesh is weak. ☐

   What are some of the barriers or problems that prevent you from rebuking your children properly?

   _____
   _____
   _____

NOTES AND COMMENTS

5. MacDonald notes that in making a rebuke, "the effective father will weigh the contents, circumstances and consequences of what he is about to say" (p. 91). What are some key questions he suggests we should ask ourselves when we rebuke our children?

_____

_____

_____

_____

6. What is the difference between a rebuke and a punishment? _____

_____

7. Remember Eli? When it came time for God to pronounce judgment on his family, we gained some insight on the importance God placed on the need for rebuking. Look up 1 Samuel 3:13 and list the two reasons for which God brought judgment on Eli's house.

A. _____

B. _____

8. In closing this chapter, MacDonald specifies on page 94 both a place and a target for a rebuke.

The place: _____

The target: _____

9. Identify one specific thing from this chapter you can apply to be more effective in rebuking your children.

_____

_____

_____

_____

NOTES AND COMMENTS

9 Wear Shoes You Want Filled

"In a previous chapter we talked about the importance of teaching to develop *abilities and standards of performance.* Now we concentrate mainly on the breeding of *attitudes and values.* More than any other way, this is done through the lifestyle of the effective father" (p. 102).

"Like it or not, a father makes impressions upon his children with far more than words. His behavior, the pattern of conduct in his own life becomes both documentation and justification for anything an offspring wishes to do" (pp. 100, 101).

Do you agree with this?

Yes ☐ No ☐ Give me a moment, I'm still trying to get my head out of the sand. ☐

2. Reflect for a moment on your exposure to your children today (or yesterday). What did they observe of your character? Your spiritual qualities?

_____

_____

_____

3. If your actions or behavior from the above would actually be imitated by your children and you could relive that time, would you do it differently?

Yes ☐ No ☐ Don't rush me, I'm still thinking. ☐

4. The conclusion of this chapter is that you are wearing the shoes that will be filled. Make sure they are the ones you want filled. As you reflect on your lifestyle, your role as a model to your children, which alternative below would represent your response to your children?

NOTES AND COMMENTS

_____
_____
_____
_____
_____
_____
_____

⬧ "Be imitators of me, as I am of Christ" (1 Corinthians 11:1).
Dr. Howard Hendricks comments on this verse, "You may be inclined to feel, 'I could never say that.' But it doesn't matter—your children are following you. The question is whether you're following Christ."

_____
_____
_____
_____
_____
_____
_____
_____
_____
_____

⬧ "The worth of a man is the yield on his father's careful investment of time."
                                    —Anonymous

_____
_____
_____

A. ☐ "I urge you, then, be imitators of me"
  (1 Corinthians 4:16).
B. ☐ "Do what I say, not what I do."
C. ☐ "Don't do anything, I'm still trying to get my
  act together."
D. ☐ "I wish you could see me twenty-four hours a
  day, because the times you do see me, I'm tired
  and irritable."

5. What specific changes in your lifestyle would you deem
necessary before you could make the same exhortation
Paul makes in 1 Corinthians 4:16, above?

_____

_____

_____

6. In 1 Corinthians 11:1 Paul shares the key ingredient to
such an exhortation. What is this ingredient?

_____

_____

7. On page 101, MacDonald highlights the basic pattern
of Paul and Timothy's relationship as shown in
2 Timothy 3:10, 11. The issue is that Timothy didn't
just hear or read about Paul's lifestyle, he *observed* it.

What specifically did Timothy observe? List those ten
areas below from these verses and assess your situation
against them. Have your children observed you in
these areas?

	Timothy observed Paul	Have your children observed this area in you?
A.	_____	Yes ☐ No ☐
B.	_____	Yes ☐ No ☐

NOTES AND COMMENTS

_____

_____

_____

◗ "With the bulk of a father's time now spent away from the place called home, the model of the father is being replaced by the lifestyles of school teachers, recreation directors, and child-care personnel. More often than not, children are learning major value systems in life from the horizontal peer-culture. The vertical structure is not there in adequate increments of time or intensity to do the job" (p. 102).

_____

_____

◗ "I disagree with those who say *all* conflicts should be carried on in privacy. . . . The rule in our house goes this way: we know you children will disagree on various things each day; we only ask that you try to disagree in the same way you see your father and mother do it" (p. 105).

_____

_____

_____

_____

_____

_____

_____

_____

_____

_____

_____

C. _____ Yes ☐ No ☐
D. _____ Yes ☐ No ☐
E. _____ Yes ☐ No ☐
F. _____ Yes ☐ No ☐
G. _____ Yes ☐ No ☐
H. _____ Yes ☐ No ☐
I. _____ Yes ☐ No ☐
J. _____ Yes ☐ No ☐

8. The author notes on page 102 that modeling a lifestyle demands time and opportunity. Sometimes we have to create experiences that will provide opportunities to model lifestyle. What are some experiences you can use to accomplish this?

_____
_____
_____
_____
_____

9. Relationships are another potential area for modeling. MacDonald notes that "the way in which an effective father relates to the children's mother is of incalculable significance" (p. 104). He notes several key areas of such a relationship. Read this section in the book carefully and rate yourself in the following areas:

	Dismally Poor	Weak But Improving	Average	"Not Bad"	Absolutely Outstanding
A. Affection	___	___	___	___	___
B. Conflict	___	___	___	___	___
C. Work	___	___	___	___	___
D. Playful spontaneity	___	___	___	___	___

NOTES AND COMMENTS

10. Identify one specific idea or insight from this chapter that you feel will make you a more effective "model" for your children.

_____

_____

_____

_____

_____

_____

10 No Busy Signals Here

"Among the dimensions of effective fatherhood, we have to include the indispensable ingredient of _approachability_ —that one can communicate with Dad without strenuous effort and that when he's engaged in family dialogue, he will be _open, responsive,_ and _concerned_" (p. 112).

1. Do you agree with the above statement? Yes ☐ No☐ What was the question again? ☐
2. Are you "approachable"?
   Yes ☐ No ☐ How close do you want to get? ☐

   Rate yourself. What is your "guestimate" of your approachability out of the total number of opportunities you have in an average week? Use a scale of 1-10. _____

   Just to give yourself a little more insight, ask your wife to rate you: _____

   Are you really brave? Ask your oldest child to rate you (if over eight or nine years old): _____

NOTES AND COMMENTS

_____
_____
_____

♦ ". . . Too many fathers have succumbed to the temptation to buy off their kids with money, things, organized activities—anything to get them off the parental back" (p. 113).

_____
_____
_____
_____
_____
_____
_____
_____
_____
_____
_____
_____
_____

♦ "In a pressurized world, engagements with one's children are most easily postponable" (p. 114).

_____
_____
_____
_____

3. On page 112, MacDonald introduces us to "Busy Signals." *Specifically*, what are some of the *busy signals* in your home?

_____

_____

_____

4. Is there such a thing as a "legitimate" busy signal?

_____

_____

5. On page 114 we're asked what is it that children want when they approach their fathers? What are they looking for?

_____

_____

_____

_____

6. MacDonald shares three qualities King David found in his "approachable" heavenly Father:
   A. An open and discriminating ear
   B. Unconditional acceptance
   C. A flexible response

   He goes on to list a number of reasons many fathers don't listen well (p. 118). What are some of these reasons?

_____

_____

_____

   Do you have trouble listening to your children? If so, which of the above reasons might best apply to you?

_____

_____

NOTES AND COMMENTS

◗ "The art of listening takes time, work, and prayer; it does not come by instinct. Conversely, it is inexcusable for any man to say that he does not have the gift of sensitivity. If he lacks it, it is because he has failed to work at it for reasons best known to himself" (p. 120).

_____

_____

_____

_____

_____

_____

_____

_____

◗ "As the years pass, we make the painful discovery that their understanding of success may be different from ours. . . . We mistake independent thought for rejection and even rebellion" (pp. 127, 128).

_____

_____

_____

_____

_____

_____

_____

_____

_____

_____

_____

_____

7. Effective and approachable fathers know *what* to listen for, as explained on pages 121–123. Read this section carefully and list the four specific things we need to be on the lookout for with our children.

   A. _____

   B. _____

   C. _____

   D. _____

8. "If we know *what* to listen for, do we know *when* to listen?" (p. 123). Can you identify specific times or instances when you might be more liable to hear valuable things from your children?

   _____

   _____

   _____

9. Discussing *unconditional acceptance*, MacDonald shares the Old Testament story of Isaac and his two sons, Esau and Jacob. He notes, "There's a very obvious moral to the story; when a man judges his children by external values and accepts them on that basis, he paves the way for relational chaos . . ." (p. 127).

   Are there external values, appearances, or behaviors that you have difficulty accepting in your children? If so, what?

   _____

   _____

   _____

   How are you handling this?
   - ☐ Excellent from mine and my child's perspective.
   - ☐ OK, with periodic flare-ups.
   - ☐ I'm doing all right on the outside, but having problems on the inside.
   - ☐ Dismally poor on all accounts.
   - ☐ Got any suggestions?

NOTES AND COMMENTS

_____

_____

_____

◗ "There is an ironic twist to the doctrine of approachability. The more approachable we are, the more we hasten the day when our children will need to approach us no longer. For as a father listens, accepts, and responds in an affirming manner, he enhances the quality of maturity. When the children 'dial' their father's number, they receive no busy signal. They know that he is just a call away. It makes them take greater risks in self-development and acceptance" (p. 133).

_____

_____

_____

_____

_____

_____

_____

◗ "The unapproachable father retards growth for awhile. His children seek his attention, and due to various conflicting inputs, they do not get it. They search for correction, for affirmation, for stability, and it isn't there. . . . Children under these conditions grow slowly and often unhealthfully. Psychologically and emotionally, they remain children far into biological adulthood" (p. 133).

_____

_____

_____

_____

10. The author, in addressing the above issue, suggests, "Perhaps the answer lies not in formulae, but rather in prayerful wisdom" (p. 128).

Where and how do we obtain such wisdom?
Want some help? Look up Proverbs 2:1-6 and James 1:5.

_____

_____

_____

Read James 3:13-18. List below, from verse 17, the attributes of the wisdom we receive from God.

1. _____   5. _____
2. _____   6. _____
3. _____   7. _____
4. _____   8. _____

11. The importance of not putting our children "on hold" at critical and important times is introduced on page 129. MacDonald calls it the *flexible response*, giving some examples on the next few pages of when those moments occur. Can you identify a few of these critical times that call for a flexible response?

_____

_____

_____

_____

_____

_____

_____

12. In closing the chapter, MacDonald asks a provocative question: "Why is it hard to grant to children the same forgiveness we as adults so desperately desire when we make mistakes?" (p. 132).

NOTES AND COMMENTS

Matthew 18:21-35 gives us some insight into God's perspective on that question. Using one or two sentences, summarize the conclusions from this passage of Scripture.

_____

_____

_____

13. Reflect for a moment on this chapter, review your notes, and identify one specific thing that, if implemented, will make you a more "approachable" father.

_____

_____

_____

_____

Dear Lord,

_____

_____

_____

_____

                         _____

                               Signature

THIRD PRINCIPLE

If I am an effective father . . . it is because I have sharpened my sensitivity to my family's needs, committed my inner being to God's laws, and fixed a foresightful eye on opportunities and hazards ahead. I want to make sure that every family experience builds my children up and matures them.

Reading Assignment:

Chapter 11   Life in White Water

Session Objectives:

To Establish the Need for and Importance of Foresightful Leadership in the Family

To Identify and Apply the Elements of Foresightful Leadership

NOTES AND COMMENTS

11 Life in White Water

"Entering a series of rapids is no time to begin making decisions about where the canoe should be pointed . . . you can't make effective decisions in a state of panic. There is no room for impulsive thinking. Life in the family is like life in white water: the person steering must always look ahead of the situation. No surprises allowed" (p. 140).

1. A contrast is drawn between a *foresightful* father and an *impulsive* father—which of these "styles" of family leadership most typically characterizes your style? Rate yourself (with an "X") on the following scale.

consistently impulsive ⊢——┼——┼——┼——┤ consistently foresightful

50/50

Take a few minutes to discuss this with your wife. Where does she rate you?

2. On page 143, MacDonald, in analyzing a conversation between Jesus and Peter, identifies the key elements of foresightful leadership. What are these elements?

A. _____

B. _____

C. _____

D. _____

The focus of this chapter is *foresight:* "The capacity to know one's children in terms of their situations and capabilities, the awareness of what to expect from them in each situation, and what the ultimate objective of their growing up in a family really is" (p. 143).

This definition provides the organizational framework of the chapter:

   I.   Stress limits in the family.

   II. Laws and convictions in family living.

  III. Decisions that keep you dry.

NOTES AND COMMENTS

♦ On page 143, we are told about a conversation Jesus had with Peter. This conversation is found in Luke 22:31-34.

> "The entire formula for anticipatory or foresightful leadership is found in that conversation. Jesus *knew Peter; he sensed the situation;* he was *ready to respond* to it; he was already *looking to the good* that would finally come out of it" (p. 143).

_____

_____

_____

_____

_____

_____

_____

_____

_____

♦ "Family leadership begins with a father who knows the stress-capacities of his children. This kind of information does not come simply by comparing our children with ourselves as we were at their age. Rather, it comes from studying *them* and watching *them* in action. Each one is entirely different in responses and ideals" (p. 144).

_____

_____

_____

_____

_____

_____

_____

Stress-limits in the family

3. Introducing the first item shown above, the book discusses not only the importance of knowing the stress capacities of our family, but how we can assess this dimension of our children.

   How can you determine the stress limits of your children? _____

   _____

   _____

4. MacDonald feels that the first and most significant stress capacity worth studying is your children's emotional pressures. He identifies several important sources of these pressures. Read the pertinent section carefully, reflecting on your own children and identify for each the pressure that might be most relevant to them on an individual basis, putting a check in the appropriate square if it applies. Rather than using a check, you may want to rate the degree of pressure on a scale of 0-10.

Child:	Pressure of Insecurity	Onset of Puberty	Competition and Pride	Peer Pressure	Parental Pressure	Other
	Pages 195-47	Pages 147-49	Pages 149-51	Pages 151-53		

NOTES AND COMMENTS

_____

_____

◗ "Foresightful fathers are sensitive to the fact that their teenaged offspring are fiercely pride-oriented. Girls will worry about their appearance; boys about their size. In the drive to assert their identity and integrity, they will find it very hard to admit that they are misinformed, that they are ignorant of something, or that they made a mistake. In the mind of the adolescent, failure is a final disaster that is larger than life" (pp. 150, 151).

_____

_____

_____

_____

_____

◗ "The children of the effective father face not only emotional stresses, but the tyranny of adolescent _peer pressure_. I observe that it begins to touch a human being significantly somewhere about the sixth grade level, at an age of eleven or twelve years" (p. 151).

_____

_____

_____

_____

_____

_____

_____

_____

_____

_____

_____

5. What specific action can you as a father take to help your children withstand the pressures you identified above?

_____

_____

_____

_____

_____

6. "The security need of a child is normally met by a reasonable amount of consistency in a home: consistency of schedule, stability of place, and normalcy of responsibilities and relationships" (p. 147).

   Does this describe your home and family environment?

   Yes ☐ No ☐ I'm still in the organization stage. ☐

   If it does not, what specific area needs your attention and corrective action? _____

   _____

   What are you going to do about it? _____

   _____

   When are you going to do it? _____

7. Looking at another cause of stress, we see the need for sensitivity to the struggles within the human spirit of a young person. *This is particularly pertinent to teenagers* as they wrestle with their convictions—social and spiritual.

   Is this a relevant issue in the lives of any of your children? Reread this section (pp. 155–160) carefully and see if you can identify a specific struggle your child might now be undergoing.

   _____

   _____

   _____

NOTES AND COMMENTS

◆ "If we are never taught to obey our parents, we will never learn how to obey God" (p. 167).

◆ "The world in which our children live appeals almost solely to the present: own this, do that, be what your friends want. A father is one of the only significant people in a child's life who will take the future into account. Thus, his decisions must always relate to what they are becoming. His view is long-range—'downriver'. Sometimes it's a rather lonely position. Not many men think that way" (p. 176).

◆ "The foresightful father follows laws and convictions. But he is not rigid" (p. 177).

Laws and convictions in family living

8. "Families need rules for living together—rules which are probably few in number but inviolable in observance. The man who does not believe that and allows his family to exist in an atmosphere of constant uncertainty will reap the result: an unstable home life in which relationships are undefined and probably exploited" (p. 164).

   Do you believe this? _____

9. MacDonald explains that rules fall into two categories: *laws* and *convictions*. How does he define these two terms?

   Laws: _____ _____

   _____

   _____

   Convictions: _____

   _____

   _____

10. Can you identify the specific *laws* that govern your home?

    Yes ☐ No ☐ Let's move on, this is too convicting. ☐

    Are they well enough defined and thought through that you could write them down?

    Yes ☐ No ☐ Mind your own business! ☐

    If a "family-law" surveyor came to your door and asked your wife the above questions, could she answer them? ____? Could your children? ____

    If you applied these same questions to the subject of convictions, how would you score?

    A B C D Flunk   (Circle one)

NOTES AND COMMENTS

Decisions that keep you dry

11. "When an effective father looks downriver in the life of his family he has to be prepared to make good decisions. And good decisions rely on a sound decision-making process" (p. 172).

    Beginning on page 171, MacDonald identifies four criteria of family decision making. What are they?

    A. _____

    B. _____

    C. _____

    D. _____

12. Remember those embarrassing questions we asked earlier on laws and convictions? Here's your opportunity to repent. *This week* set aside an evening to pray and interact with your wife. The purpose? . . . to *clearly identify* and *write down* the laws and convictions you believe, as a couple, should govern your family. Agreed?

    Date: _____ Time: _____

    Not so fast—you're not done yet. Schedule an additional time over the next two weeks to sit down with your children to explain the concept of laws and convictions and to communicate the ones specific to your family. When will you have this time?

    Date: _____ Time: _____

    Dear Lord,

    _____

    _____

    _____

    _____

    _____

    Signature

FOURTH PRINCIPLE

If I am an effective father . . . it is because I am filling my children's lives with perspectives and patterns which produce wisdom; I am lovingly purging their lives of unwholesome influences and tendencies that impede their progress toward maturity.

Reading Assignment:

Chapter 12   To Raise a Great Cathedral

Session Objectives:

To establish the importance of wisdom as an attribute to be developed in our children.

To identify the things a parent must give his children in order to provide the conditions for wisdom.

NOTES AND COMMENTS

_____
_____
_____
_____
_____
_____
_____
_____
_____
_____
_____

◆ "Wisdom is not a natural or instinctive characteristic. We are not born with it. It is something which is first given, then exercised, and finally mastered" (p. 185).

_____
_____
_____
_____
_____
_____
_____
_____
_____
_____
_____
_____
_____
_____

12 To Raise a Great Cathedral

1. As a father, what is your primary task and responsibility? Can you write your job description in thirty words or less?

   _____

   _____

   _____

   _____

   _____

2. "*Skill* is not a top biblical priority. The God of the Bible makes it plain that fathers are responsible to produce people of deep inner spirit. *Spirit.* not skill, is essential" (p. 184).

   Do you agree with that? _____

3. In session one we asked you to think through some of the attributes and character traits you want to see developed in your children by the time they are eighteen years old. Was wisdom one of those attributes?

   Yes ☐ No ☐ How do you spell that? ☐

4. In discussing Proverbs 8:35, 36, MacDonald concludes, "The message for fathers is simple: use those tools of fatherhood which introduce wisdom into the lives of your children because wisdom brings one's life to its fullest potential" (p. 185).

   He goes on to define this wisdom of which Solomon speaks. What is this definition?

   Wisdom is . . . _____

   _____

   _____

   _____

   _____

NOTES AND COMMENTS

Finally, the fourth paragraph on page 185 identifies some of the characteristics of a *wise* person. Reread this section carefully, underlining the paragraph.

Does this describe an attribute you want your children to have?

Like previous chapters, this one also has a specific focus—*wisdom*. After reading Proverbs and analyzing Solomon's thinking on the matter, MacDonald concludes that a parent has three things to give his children in order to provide the conditions for wisdom. As before, these conclusions give us insight into the organization of this chapter.

I. *Training.* How we shape that part of a child which produces both habit and desire.

II. *Spiritual conditioning.* Enlarging of one's capacity to act in a wise and Christlike way.

III. *Punishment.* Confronting the child with the consequences of living unwisely.

"Do it again . . . and again . . . and again . . . and . . ."

"Train up a child in the way
he should go, and when he is
old he will not depart from
it " (Proverbs 22:6).

This section deals with *what* we are training our children to do and *how* we train them to do it. For example, in training our children to develop certain habits, we use the tools of repetition, affirmation, and reinforcement.

NOTES AND COMMENTS

5. On pages 186–191, MacDonald discusses training your children in four areas: habits, reflexes, values, and ambitions/personal sense of destiny. In each area he provides definition and shares some insights into the method of training for that area, also giving some examples. Read this section carefully and complete the questions below. Try to identify at least one training need for each of your children; and for that need, think through the specific action or training method most applicable. An example in the area of *habits* is provided to get you started.

	Training need for my child(ren)	Training Method
		Repetition, affirmation, and reinforcement
Habits (p. 189) Daily activities which become so common- place that we no longer have to think deliber- ately about do- ing them.	*e.g., orderliness*	
Reflexes (p. 189) Forms of auto- matic be- havior in re- sponse to situ- ations around us.		
Values (p. 190) Intrinsic assign- ments of relative worth we place on principles,		

NOTES AND COMMENTS

_____

_____

_____

_____

_____

_____

_____

_____

_____

_____

_____

_____

◗ "Discipline helps children learn that feelings do not run their lives. Fluctuating moods, fatigue, ignorance, and even some types of pain will limit us to substandard performance if we allow them to do so" (p. 195).

_____

_____

_____

_____

_____

_____

_____

_____

_____

_____

_____

concepts, ideas, _____ _____
things, etc., that _____ _____
provide criteria _____ _____
by which we _____ _____
make decisions. _____ _____

Ambitions, per- _____ _____
sonal sense of des- _____ _____
tiny (p. 191) _____ _____
   The self-esteem _____ _____
   a father gives _____ _____
   his children, _____ _____
   which in turn _____ _____
   makes them con- _____ _____
   scious of the _____ _____
   potential _____ _____

Pain makes the person

Remember the second item we need to give our children in order to provide the conditions for wisdom? *Spiritual conditioning.* There's another term for this—*discipline.*

"When a father disciplines his children, he is enlarging their capacity to endure and produce" (p. 193).

6. How does MacDonald define discipline on page 194? __
_____
_____
_____

7. What is the difference between discipline and punishment? _____
_____
_____
_____

NOTES AND COMMENTS

_____

_____

_____

_____

_____

_____

_____

_____

_____

_____

◗ "Is what I am doing really punishment? Or am I simply taking out my frustrations upon someone smaller than I—someone who won't fight back . . . at least for now? It could be that the punishment is actually vengeance or just anger that I have been let down by my kids" (p. 197).

_____

_____

_____

_____

_____

_____

_____

_____

_____

_____

_____

_____

8. What is the purpose of discipline? _____

   _____

   _____

9. Grab your Bible and find Hebrews 12. Carefully read
   verses 4 through 13. Write out verse 11 in the space
   provided here.

   _____

   _____

   _____

   _____

It really does hurt me more than it hurts you

Here we are introduced to *punishment*, a way of confronting the child with the consequences of living unwisely.

10. On pages 197, 198, MacDonald identifies two dif-
    ferent patterns of punishment, *corrective* punishment
    and *judicial* punishment. How are these two forms of
    punishment defined?
    Corrective punishment: _____

    _____

    Judicial punishment: _____

    _____

11. Now we are introduced to a very important but
    sometimes controversial area. Beginning on page 206,
    MacDonald discusses seven key rules or principles of
    punishment. What are these principles? Take the time
    to write them below; this will help you remember
    them.

    1. _____

       _____

NOTES AND COMMENTS

◗ "Solomon seems to be contradicting the unconscious hope many fathers have that their children will 'grow out' of their rebellion as they mature. They won't!" (p. 202).

_____
_____
_____
_____
_____
_____
_____
_____
_____
_____
_____
_____
_____
_____
_____
_____
_____
_____
_____
_____
_____
_____
_____
_____
_____

2. _____
   _____
3. _____
   _____
4. _____
   _____
5. _____
   _____
6. _____
   _____
7. _____
   _____

Which of the above principles do you feel you must consistently apply?

Which of the above principles do you feel identifies a weak area in your punishment practices or provides a new insight you haven't considered before? Circle it.

A note of encouragement:

There are two essential elements in becoming an effective father—an *understanding* of the principles of being such a father and the *application* of these principles within the fabric and context of your family. Neither of these two key elements can work without the other.

MacDonald shares many of these principles. You are responsible for the application. Only as we turn principle into practice will we become effective fathers.

12. Review question 5 in this discussion chapter and identify at least one specific training need for each of your children. This can be from any of the areas discussed (habits, reflexes, values and ambitions). Write

NOTES AND COMMENTS

_____
_____
_____
_____
_____
_____
_____
_____
_____
_____
_____
_____
_____
_____
_____
_____
_____

that need down as well as the specific action (training tool or method) you will take to meet it.

Training Needed: _____ Action: _____

_____ _____

_____ _____

13. Does your wife share in the responsibility for punishment in your home? Set aside a specific time this week for sharing and interaction with her on the seven principles of punishment you identified earlier in this chapter. When will you do this?

Date: _____ Time: _____

Dear Lord,

_____

_____

_____

_____

_____

Signature

FIFTH
PRINCIPLE

If I am an effective father . . . it is
because I accept and affirm my
children for who they are, appreciate them for what they are accomplishing, and cover them with
affection because they are mine.

Reading Assignment:

Chapter 13   Please Show Me That You Care

Session Objectives:

To establish the importance of approval by us as fathers to
our children.
To explore several creative ways of expressing approval to our
children.

NOTES AND COMMENTS

_____

_____

_____

_____

_____

_____

_____

◗ What is the difference between appreciation and affirmation?

"You appreciate an action—you affirm a gift."
—Gordon MacDonald

For example:

Appreciation: "I appreciated it when you encouraged me when I was down."

Affirmation: "You have the gift of being able to tell when people are down and knowing how to encourage them."

_____

_____

_____

_____

_____

_____

_____

_____

_____

_____

_____

13 Please Show Me That You Care

"Approval by significant people in our lives is a funda-
mental need. Our composite health—physical, emotional
and spiritual—cannot survive without it" (p. 218).

1. Do you agree with the above statement? Reflect for a
   moment on your own childhood. How would you rate
   your father on the following "approval" scale?

   Consistently
   dissatisfied ├──────────────┴──────────────┤ Consistently
   and critical   50/50   approving

   How would you rate yourself as a father? How would
   your wife rate you on the above scale?

2. This chapter identifies a number of ways a father ex-
   tends approval to his children: *affirmation, appreciation,
   and affection*. On page 223 affirmation is introduced.
   How is it defined?

   _____

   _____

3. What is the difference between affirmation and appreciation? _____

   _____

   _____

4. MacDonald notes, "As fathers we must know not only
   how to affirm our children but *when* and *for what* pur-
   poses" (p. 224). In establishing the need for sensitivity,
   he asks some very challenging questions. Can you answer them for your children?

   A. What does your child want to do? _____

      _____

      _____

      _____

NOTES AND COMMENTS

_____

_____

_____

_____

_____

While illustrating the importance of parental approval, MacDonald outlines the following behavioral pattern:

Parent says or conveys	→ Dissatisfaction and criticism	"You could have done it better . . . faster . . . easier."
Child feels	→ Low self-esteem	The personal conviction that one is useless and worthless.
Child's reaction	→ Withdrawal or overachievement	

ceasing to pursue any form of excellence → insatiable appetite for prominence and recognition.

_____

_____

◗ "The appreciated child is an adjusted child, happy with his place in the family. He is aware that he really counts" (p. 228).

_____

_____

_____

_____

_____

_____

_____

_____

B. What does he/she do best? _____

_____

_____

_____

C. How does he/she need approval? _____

_____

_____

_____

_____

D. What qualities of character and personality do you see that need to be highlighted and praised so that your children know you consider them important?

_____

_____

_____

_____

"As affirmation concentrates on what a child is, *appreciation* highlights what a child has done" (p. 227).

5. Children need to be appreciated for the contribution they make to our lives—to the family's welfare. Can you think of a single but meaningful contribution each of your children makes to your family?

_____

_____

_____

_____

What creative ways can you use to express your appreciation? _____

_____

_____

_____

NOTES AND COMMENTS

_____

_____

_____

▶ "Many fathers unconsciously begin to withdraw from their daughters when they notice the first signs of puberty. . . . Research reveals that girls who enter into promiscuous sexual relationships at an early age almost always come from homes where fathers have been unaffectionate and have failed to meet the need of their young daughters to be touched and physically affirmed" (p. 231).

_____

_____

_____

_____

_____

_____

_____

_____

_____

_____

_____

_____

_____

_____

_____

_____

_____

_____

"*Affection*, the nonverbal communication of closeness, touching, and stroking is among the most important experiences we share with one another" (p. 229).

6. On pages 229, 230, MacDonald discusses the different roles touching plays in the life of your children, noting that the meaning changes as your children grow. What are these roles?

_____

_____

_____

7. As children grow, not only the *forms* of affection change; so do the appropriate times. This is particularly pertinent for teenagers. Pride and peer pressure frequently create a gap between what is *accepted* versus what is *needed*.

Have you found this to be true in your home? What are some creative ways you can use to express needed affection without violating what is acceptable to your child and his peer group?

_____

_____

_____

_____

_____

_____

8. The focus of this chapter has been the fifth of six principles MacDonald shares with us for effective fatherhood.

> If I am an effective father . . . it is because I accept and affirm my children for who they are, appreciate them for what they are accomplishing, and cover them with affection because they are mine.

NOTES AND COMMENTS

_____
_____
_____
_____
_____
_____
_____
_____
_____
_____
_____
_____
_____
_____
_____

Reflect for a moment on the key points learned in this chapter. What specific action will you take this week that will allow you to more effectively apply this principle?

_____

_____

_____

_____

_____

Dear Lord,

_____

_____

_____

_____

_____

                                     Signature

SIXTH PRINCIPLE

If I am an effective father . . . it is because I am aware that I always live on the edge of ineffectiveness and must continually reach out to God for wisdom and skill to accomplish my task.

Reading Assignment:

Chapter 14　The Sour Hour—the Ineffective Father

Session Objectives:

To identify what to do when what you've done doesn't work.
To develop an understanding of the role of your wife and church in your role as a father.
To identify the essential ingredient of effective fatherhood.

NOTES AND COMMENTS

_____

_____

_____

_____

_____

_____

_____

_____

_____

_____

_____

_____

_____

◗ "At best, the effective father will have fifteen years to set the style, and the first eight are the most important. After that—and I am already being generous—we can hope at best to make minor mid-course corrections " (p. 102).

_____

_____

_____

_____

_____

_____

_____

_____

_____

_____

14 The Sour Hour—The Ineffective Father

We've spent several weeks studying and discussing the principles for effective fatherhood. We have been evaluating our role as fathers and attempting to integrate these new insights and principles into our day-to-day family responsibilities.

The stage is set—the book has been read, the principles identified, the concepts discussed; commitments have been made, and prayers prayed.

In our mind's eye we see ourselves operating as fathers in a manner that can only be characterized as *par excellence*. We see ourselves applying these principles with such impact that neighbors line up on our doorstep to discover the secrets of our success.

Then the phenomenon—identified by MacDonald in this chapter, as the sour hour—appears and quickly brings us back to reality. In spite of all of our study, prayer, and commitment—something goes wrong.

"Are there any families which have not experienced crises when everything seemed to disintegrate? . . . Tension fills the air; sullenness, anger, and distance are the order of the day. 'What have I done wrong?' a father asks. 'And what do I do now?'" (p. 240).

Have you experienced a sour hour?

Yes □ No □ I gave at the office. □

On pages 245–247 MacDonald introduces us to several types of defeated parents:

> bitter and disillusioned
> sad and bewildered
> defiant

NOTES AND COMMENTS

◆ "As far as the east is from the west, so far does he re-
move our transgressions from us" (Psalm 103:12).

_____

_____

_____

_____

_____

_____

_____

_____

◆ "'For this my son was dead, and is alive again; he was
lost, and is found.' And they began to make merry" (Luke
15:24).

_____

_____

_____

_____

_____

_____

_____

_____

_____

_____

_____

_____

_____

_____

These are parents of adolescent children who are living in prolonged rebellion, whose sour hours have extended to sour days, sour months, and even sour years.

"Faced with the consequences of failure most defeated fathers will do almost anything. But what is up for grabs is the response of the children. The chances are that the children will not respond to a father's remorse or efforts of reconciliation" (p. 247).

What comfort is there for a parent who is confronted with the fruit of past parental performance? Where the relationship between parent and child is broken and immediate restoration may not be realized? MacDonald shares his thoughts in the next few pages.

FIRST   —Affirmation of God's forgiveness to the defeated parent—such forgiveness does not obviate the consequences of past action but guarantees a fresh and life-giving rightness with God.

SECOND—Children remain under God's care—"What is impossible with men is possible with God" (Luke 18:27).

On page 249, MacDonald shares some insights about the parable of the "Prodigal Son." This is the story of a father who, through God's grace, was able to deal successfully with a severed relationship under difficult circumstances.

In 1 Corinthians 13:4-8 Paul shares some of the attributes of a special type of love which are listed below. Carefully read the parable, found in Luke 15:11-32, and check the characteristics of love below that you feel the father of the prodigal son displayed, explaining your reasons in the space provided.

☐ Love is patient: ——————————————

☐ is kind: ——————————————

NOTES AND COMMENTS

_____

_____

_____

_____

_____

_____

_____

_____

_____

_____

_____

_____

_____

_____

◗ "Finally, brethren, whatever is true, whatever is honorable, whatever is just, whatever is pure, whatever is lovely, whatever is gracious, if there is any excellence, and if there is anything worthy of praise, think about these things" (Philippians 4:8).

_____

_____

_____

_____

_____

_____

_____

_____

_____

☐ is not jealous: _____

☐ does not brag: _____

☐ is not arrogant: _____

☐ does not act unbecomingly: _____

☐ does not seek its own: _____

☐ is not provoked: _____

☐ does not take into account a
wrong suffered: _____

☐ does not rejoice in unrighteousness: _____

☐ rejoices with truth: _____

☐ bears all things: _____

☐ believes all things: _____

☐ hopes all things: _____

☐ endures all things: _____

☐ Love never fails: _____

Does the type of love described above characterize your life?

_____

_____

How does one allow this kind of love to develop and grow in his life?

_____

_____

THIRD—God has an amazing network of his people around the world that he might use to correct the course set by wayward and lost offspring.

Have you ever been used by the Lord in this type of situation?

_____

_____

NOTES AND COMMENTS

◗ "Do not rejoice in failures, but affirm successes. Love, Love, Love!" (p. 251).

◗ Want a blessing? Read Proverbs 31:10-31.

A good wife who can find?
She is far more precious than jewels (v. 10).

She opens her mouth with wisdom,
and the teaching of kindness is on her tongue (v. 26).

Her children rise up and call her blessed;
her husband also, and he praises her:
"Many women have done excellently,
but you surpass them all" (vv. 28, 29).

FOURTH—Prepare yourself for the moment when you will be needed again.

On page 251, the author gives valuable insights on the perspective a parent must have to be available and of use when the need arises. Summarize this perspective in your own words:

_____

_____

_____

_____

_____

Last, MacDonald asks the question,

"Can I be an effective father by myself? No," he responds, there are some additional ingredients needed.

1. A healthy and productive relationship with your wife.
2. A meaningful fellowship with your church.
3. A personal relationship with Jesus Christ.

What is the role your wife should play in helping you become a more effective father?

_____

_____

_____

_____

How does she view this role?

_____

_____

_____

_____

NOTES AND COMMENTS

▶ "Let us consider how to stir up one another to love and good works, not neglecting to meet together, as is the habit of some, but encouraging one another, and all the more as you see the Day drawing near" (Hebrews 10:24, 25).

_____

_____

_____

_____

_____

_____

_____

▶ "I came that they may have life, and have it abundantly" (Jesus Christ; John 10:10).

_____

_____

_____

_____

_____

_____

▶ "For God so loved the world that he gave his only Son, that whoever believes in him should not perish but have eternal life" (John 3:16).

_____

_____

_____

_____

Have you sat down as a couple and discussed this aspect of your marriage?

Yes ☐ No ☐ I'm glad you asked that question— ☐
          we're planning on doing it tonight.

What role should your church play in helping you with your parenting task?

_____

_____

_____

Is it meeting this need? If not, how could it?

_____

_____

In closing this last chapter, MacDonald notes . . . "It is the power of Jesus Christ, therefore, that makes me capable of carrying out all the principles I have mentioned. It is he who, having changed my life and started me on the process of daily spiritual maturity, sends me home to be an effective father. Without him I cannot find the energy I need to implement the principles of effective fatherhood" (p. 255).

How do we receive this power Christ provides for effective living—for effective fatherhood?

The New Testament gives us the answer to this important question—this power is the result of a personal relationship with a living person, the Lord Jesus Christ.

John 1:12 provides insight as to how this relationship is established—

"To as many as received him to them he gave the right to become the children of God, even to them that believe on his name."

NOTES AND COMMENTS

_____

_____

_____

_____

_____

_____

_____

_____

_____

_____

_____

_____

◗ "But God shows his love for us in that while we were yet sinners Christ died for us" (Paul; Romans 5:8).

_____

_____

_____

_____

_____

_____

_____

_____

_____

_____

Notice there are three operative verbs in this statement: *believe, receive, become.* Someone has said that in becoming a Christian there is *something* to be believed and *someone* to be received.

Belief is not enough—one must believe in Jesus Christ *and* personally receive him into his life to become a child of God.

Mere intellectual assent to facts does not make a person a Christian anymore than mere intellectual assent to facts makes a person married.

It is obvious that merely believing in a woman, however intense that belief may be, does not make one married. If, in addition, we are emotionally involved with that woman we still will not be married. One finally has to come to a commitment of the will and say, "I do," receiving the other person into his life and committing himself to the other person, thereby establishing the relationship. It involves total commitment of intellect, emotions, and will.

Just as getting married means giving up our independence, so does receiving Christ. The essence of *sin* is living independently of God—going my way rather than his way.

This independence from God is not a unique problem— casual observations of our world provide ample evidence of this independence, of this sin. The Bible also makes this clear.

". . . all have sinned and fall short of the glory of God" (Romans 3:23).

"For the wages of sin is death [spiritual separation from God]" (Romans 6:23).

The essence of repentance is the repudiation of this self-centered principle, making Christ and his will the center of my life.

How then do we actually receive Jesus Christ?

NOTES AND COMMENTS

◆ "I am the way, and the truth, and the life; no one comes to the Father, but by me" (Jesus Christ; John 14:6).

_____

_____

_____

_____

_____

_____

_____

_____

_____

_____

_____

_____

_____

_____

_____

_____

_____

_____

_____

_____

_____

_____

_____

_____

_____

_____

_____

_____

In Revelation 3:20, Jesus compares our lives to a house and says:

> "Behold, I stand at the door and knock; if any one hears my voice and opens the door, I will come in to him and eat with him, and he with me."

The Lord Jesus Christ is knocking at the door of your life. He will not gate-crash or force his way in, but will come in only at your invitation.

This invitation can be given him simply in our own words in prayer.

Prayer is merely talking with God. God knows your heart and is not as concerned with your words as he is with the attitude of your heart.

Many have used a prayer somewhat like this.

> Lord Jesus, I need you. Thank you for dying on the cross for my sins. I open the door of my life and receive you as my Savior and Lord. Thank you for forgiving my sins and giving me eternal life. Take control of the throne of my life. Make me the kind of person you want me to be.

Does this prayer express the desire of your heart? Would you like to have a personal relationship with Jesus Christ, the living God—the Lord of the universe?

If you desire this relationship, pray this prayer right now and Christ will come into your life as he promised.

"The effective father is, above all things, a man touched by the power of Jesus Christ" (p. 254).

Review your study and discussion notes. Can you identify one specific point of application—one thing under each principle that you are doing differently, as a father, as a result of your time and study in this book? In summary

NOTE: Some of the above material was taken from *How to Give Away Your Faith* by Paul Little (© 1966 Inter-Varsity Christian Fellowship). Used by permission of InterVarsity Press.

NOTES AND COMMENTS

and for review, write these points of application under each of the respective principles below.

If I am an effective father . . . it is because:

I. I have deliberately set as one of my life's highest priorities the creation of conditions in my home that will stimulate my children to grow to their full human potential.

_____

_____

_____

_____

_____

_____

_____

_____

_____

II. I have devoted myself to become an instrument, a model of human experience to my children.

_____

_____

_____

_____

_____

_____

_____

_____

III. I have sharpened my sensitivity to my family's needs, committed my inner being to God's laws, and fixed a foresightful eye on opportunities and hazards ahead. I

NOTES AND COMMENTS

want to make sure that every family experience builds my children up and matures them.

IV. I am filling my children's lives with perspectives and patterns which produce wisdom; I am lovingly purging their lives of unwholesome influences and tendencies that impede their progress toward maturity.

V. I accept and affirm my children for who they are, appreciate them for what they are accomplishing, and cover them with affection because they are mine.

NOTES AND COMMENTS

VI. I am aware that I always live on the edge of ineffectiveness and must continually reach out to God for
wisdom and skill to accomplish my task.

_____

_____

_____

_____

_____

_____

_____

Dear Lord,

_____

_____

_____

_____

_____

Signature